Wind Dance

Ellen Bryan Obed

illustrated by Shawn Steffler

SCHOLASTIC CANADA LTD.

Many of these poems and the art originally appeared in *Wind in My Pocket*, published by Breakwater Books, 1990.

Canadian Cataloguing in Publication Data

Obed, Ellen Bryan, 1944-
  Wind dance

Poems.
ISBN 1-55268-229-3

I. Steffler, Shawn, 1950- . II. Title.

PS8579.B43W56 1999   jC811'.54   C98-932879-1
PR9199.3.O23W56 1999

5 4 3   Printed and bound in Canada   05 06 07 08

for the children of
Newfoundland
Labrador
and the Quebec North Shore

and for my uncle
Robert A. Bryan
who first introduced me to them

Summer Reading

I read a book this summer when we traveled to the shore.
I read it in the car till I reached page twenty-four.

I read it in the boat to the motor's steady hum,
Until the water splashed and sprayed on page thirty-one.

I read it on the beach when we got ourselves to land.
Now page forty-seven is speckled brown with sand.

I read it with an ice cream in the hot and melting sun,
When drops of sticky chocolate fell on page fifty-one.

I read it in a hammock when a spider from the tree
Came down and crawled across the words on page sixty-three.

I read it by the fire roasting marshmallows quite late.
Now page eighty-seven sticks to page eighty-eight.

I read it in my sleeping bag (no one could see the light).
I read until I'd finished in the middle of the night.

Then I read the last page over, and over one more time,
Until my head dropped down to sleep on page niney-nine!

Ribbon Seller's Song

Ribbons, ribbons, plenty of ribbons!
Will anyone buy from me
    Ribbons of sunlight,
    Ribbons of seaweed,
Ribbons of bark from the tree?

Ribbons, ribbons, I sell ribbons.
Will anyone stop to buy
    Ribbons of rootlets,
    Ribbons of rainbows,
Ribbons of cloud from the sky?

Grass Song

Witchgrass, stitchgrass, in-the-roadside-ditch grass;
Junegrass, strewn grass, waving-on-the-dune grass;
    Everywhere I pass, grass. Everywhere I see

Bluegrass, new grass, wet-with-morning-dew grass;
Sniff grass, stiff grass, growing-on-the-cliff grass;
    Everywhere I pass, grass. Everywhere I see

Fox-tail, squirrel-tail, standing-brown-and-stale grass;
Barley, timothy, tickles-on-the-knee grass;
    Everywhere I pass, grass. Everywhere I see

Clump grass, stump grass, even-in-the-dump grass;
Moose grass, goose grass, anyone can use grass;
Sweet grass, peat grass — we can even EAT grass!
    Everywhere I pass, grass — and grasses pass me!

The River

The river is a long and quiet place to be,
Wide and contented, moving to the sea.
Of slow tide and dark bank and tired stone —
Far from its white streams, deep and alone.
Wide and contented, moving to the sea;
The river is a long and quiet place to be.

I Love Rain —

the still and gray before of rain,
the comes-a-little-more of rain,
the one-drop-in-my-eye of rain
that's coming from the sky of rain.

I love rain —

the easy come and go of rain,
the changing fast and slow of rain,
the all-around-me-mist of rain,
the quick wind's lively twist of rain.

I love rain —

the all-things-getting-wet of rain,
the sounds we can't forget of rain,
the rain that comes again of rain,
the rainy raining rain of rain.

I love rain.

Rhubarb

Long the fishing place abandoned,
Long the houses grey and still,
Long the gravestones dim and leaning,
But the rhubarb by the hill
Straight and high as if the pickers
Soon would pull the stalks aside —
Some for sauce and some for puddings,
Some for summer supper pies.

Pals

Charles is my pal,
I'm his chum.
But Charles chews cherries
And I chew gum.

Charles plays checkers,
I like to chat.
Charles chases chipmunks,
I chase the cat.

Charles has chickens,
I keep bees.
Charles likes chips,
I choose cheese.

Charles chews cherries,
I chew gum.
But Charles is my pal
And I'm his chum.

The Storm

grumbles
from
far
and far away;
moves
closer,
burdened,
bold and grey

stumbles
and cracks
his crooked cane;
scattering
fast
and frightened
rain;

chases
us in
until he is gone
far away
stumbling,
grumbling on.

Wind Song

"When one is in love with the Wind, Mother,
When one cannot sleep for its blow,
When all one can feel are its arms, Mother;
When one loves the Wind, does it know?

Yes, I am in love with the Wind, Mother,
And all I can hear or can see
Or feel or want is the Wind, Mother;
Do you think the Wind also loves me?"

There Once Was a Man Down the Bay

There once was a man down the bay
Who wanted black hair — not gray —
    So he decided to use
    Some blackberry juice,

But his hair became purple that day.

Now this gentleman man was so vain
That none dared to mention the stain
    That ran down his cheeks
    In purplish streaks
Whenever it started to rain.

Bonfire Night

One by one the bonfires come
Snapping loud and leaping high —
Orange dancers in the night
With grey scarves twirling in the sky.

One by one the bonfires go
Stepping slowly out of sight,
Long grey scarves about their arms —
Tired dancers in the night.

Moon

Giant Cookie
baked in Oven Sun,
I will run
away with you
when you are done
and eat you
in Night's closet
and taste
your sugared stars
upon my tongue.

"When Ye Goes"

"Winter will come when ye goes, Miss,
Though spring has just gone away.
the current is cold from the floes, Miss,
And snow's on the hills in the bay.

The sky will git grey as the rocks, Miss;
The dogs will be mocking the blow
Of the wind and asking it loud, Miss,
When it's bringing its bullwhips of snow.

When ye goes away to your place, Miss,
Do ye think o' the summer again?
When winter is long in our land, Miss,
We talks o' the sound o' the plane."

Snowbirds

A gust
of lively
snowflakes fell.
(I thought
that Winter
knew them well.)
But when
they rose
in restless flight,
somehow
something
wasn't right.

Against
the sun and
down the sky
I watch
them make
another try.

I see
them feathered
in the wind —
snowbirds
in our land
again.

Winter Journey

In goose-down fields
    we leave our tracks
while black-crow cliffs
    look down our backs.
Over porcupine hills
    we make our way
to the red fox sun
    on the side of day.

Arctic Fox

White as the white of snow on snow,
He curls in the whirls of the arctic blow;
We can't see him sleep and can't see him go —
White as the white of snow on snow.

Cold

I am cold, cold, cold, cold, COLD, COLD, COLD
    and nothing is keeping me warm —
    Not my cap or my sweater
    or my mittens make it better
    in the very cold, cold of the storm.

I am cold, cold, cold, cold, COLD, COLD, COLD,
    shivering and quivering with chill —
    and my scarf won't suffice
    though it's wrapped around me twice.
    I am very, very VERY cold still.

I am cold, cold, cold, cold, COLD, COLD, COLD
    (Very soon I think I'm going to freeze!)
    though the jacket that I'm in
    is zipped up to my chin
    and my socks are pulled up to my knees!

I'm cold, cold, cold, cold, COLD, COLD, COLD.
    Will I ever (no, I'll never) be warm?
    For the COLD, COLD, COLD
    keeps me cold, cold, cold
    in the very cold, cold of the storm.

Winter Reading

I curl up
in Winter's lap
and listen
to her icy tales.
I shiver
and I cannot sleep
though round
she wraps
her blanket deep
and keeps
a sliver of a light
through the dark
chapters of the night.

Blizzard

The night is so wild with snow
I fear the world might lose its way
And fall back into yesterday,
Or race so fast instead
Tumble several days ahead.
And I would be left standing by
In a house of wind and a roof of sky!

Winter Choice

This shovel,
That shovel,
Which one shall I choose
to shovel
shining chunks of snow
from the shingles
on my roof?

This shovel,
That shovel,
I shall put them back.
I can't shovel
chunks of snow
from the shingles
on my shack.

This wind,
That wind,
I shall ask instead,
"Please blow
the chunks of snow
from the shingles
on my shed."

When

When will the ice break up in the north?
When will the boats whish up to the wharf?
When will the white of snow disappear?
When will the geese whistle green the year?
When will the whale whirl up the sea?
When will the wind whisper warm to me?

The Skate

The ice is thick.
The ice is thin.
If I skate,
Will I fall in?

Temperature down,
Sun up high.
Spiral and spin,
I think I'll try.

Thick is thick.
Thin is thin.
When I went out,
I went in!

North Dance

Dance sea
on dark cliff
hard and high;
dance gull
in sea salt
shaking sky.
Dance spruce
in forest
black and tight;
dance day
with long leaps
in the night.
dance fly
in tiny,
spitting swarm;
dance melt
down mountain
in the warm.
Dance frost
on berries
ripening low;
dance cold
with wind and
snow with snow.

Sky Carver

Genty the sun
with steady eye
whittled at winter
from the sky.

Deeper she cut
with sharpened ray
as pieces of winter
fell away.

Warmly she held
it up when done,
"This is my carving called Spring,"
said the Sun.

The White Ships

No mother leans to the window glass;
No eager children wait the bow;
No dogs wake hungry on the rocks
to meet the ships that enter now.

They come — the white ships of the spring —
Built far north of the Labrador.
The Sea, their captain, brings them in
To sun and quiet tide, their shore.

In Cloud Land

We can run
down long cloud paths
    and climb
the tall cloud mountains.
    We can jump
from high cloud cliffs
    and swim
the deep cloud oceans.
    We can sit
on small cloud hills
    and watch
the cloud birds soaring
    and go to sleep
on soft cloud beds
    and dream
cloud dreams 'til morning.

The Robin Sang

The robin sang
with his red breast high.
He sang loud and late
to the red-breast sky.

The robin sang
'til the spruce was black.
He sang to the sky
with its cloud-feathered back.

The robin was still
when the sky was gone.
Dark in the spruce,
he sat alone.

The robin sang
with his red breast high
when early again
came the red-breast sky.

Wind in my Pocket

With wind in my pocket up from the sea
    and a cloud from the sky to wear,
With a bundle of sun tucked under my arm
    and ribbons of rain in my hair,
I walked to a bend in the afternoon
    for a friend who was waiting there.